Steve Parish

KIDS

I SPY

The Magpie

"Help your children learn the names of animals common in Australian backyards."

Aa

"I Spy" is a magpie with very sharp eyes.
He sits on top of the fence in my backyard and watches the world go by.

apple

ant

On Monday I Spy broke into **a** long rolling song, so beautiful that **all** the **ants** stopped eating their **apples and** listened contentedly.

ankle

axe

Bb

On Tuesday I Spy's song was so loud that all of the **Bunyips** were **blown** out of the **barn**, never to return again.

Can you see any **Bunyips** in the **barn**?

See, I told you!

brown  butterfly

TUESDAY

WHERE DID ALL THOSE BUNYIPS GO?

barn

bird

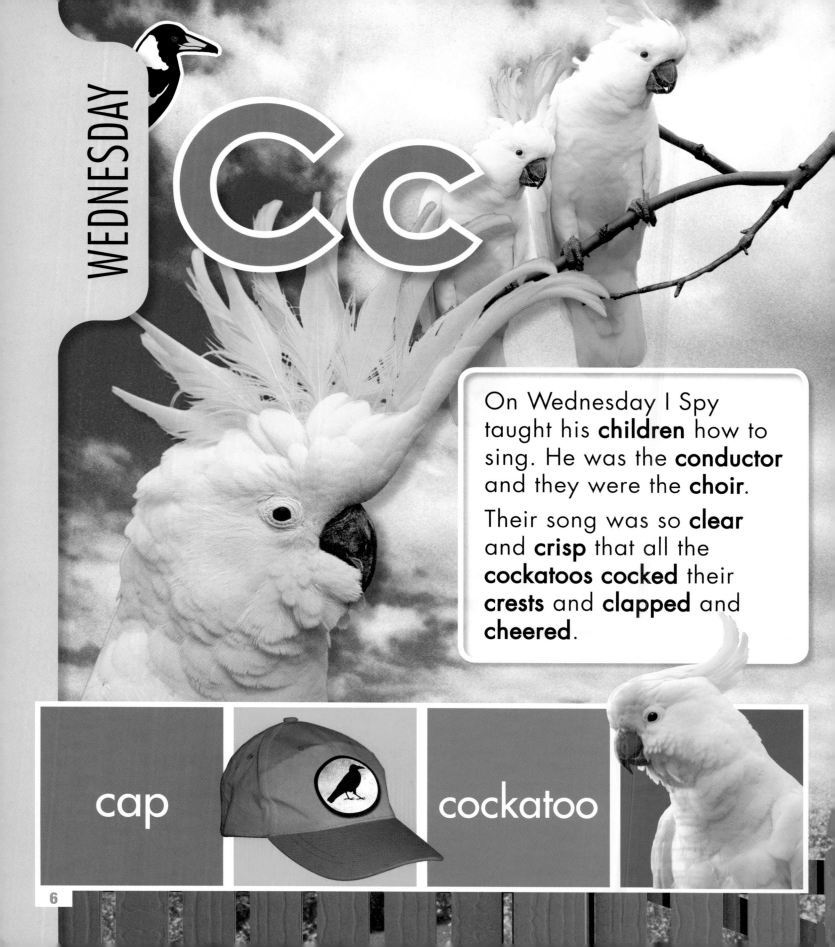

Cc

On Wednesday I Spy taught his **children** how to sing. He was the **conductor** and they were the **choir**.

Their song was so **clear** and **crisp** that all the **cockatoos cocked** their **crests** and **clapped** and **cheered**.

cap

cockatoo

crest

cat

Dd

On Thursday I Spy sang so sweetly that the **dogs** stopped to listen, the **daisies** danced and swayed and all the **dragons** turned into **dragonflies**!

If you don't believe me, try to find a **dragon** in your backyard.

They've all gone but there are always lots of **dragonflies**!

dog

dragonfly

THURSDAY

dragon

daisy

Ee

On Friday I Spy's songs made all the **eggs** hatch into **echidnas.**

It's true! **Echidnas** hatch from **eggs** and I Spy saw them with his very keen **eye**!

echidna

egg

Ff

On **Friday** the **feather-tails** were **fascinated** but …

… the **frogs** almost **fainted** at the sound of I Spy's voice.

flower

frog

Gg

On Saturday when I Spy sang, all the **geckoes** were **gobsmacked** and couldn't speak a word.

You try **getting** a **gecko** to talk on a Saturday!

grass

gecko

SATURDAY

Hh

THAT'S NOT MY HONEY-EATING HAT! IT'S TOO BIG!

All the **honeyeaters** lost their **hats. Honest!** Even with I Spy and his very sharp eye, they couldn't find their **honey-eating hats** again.

hat

honey

Ii

On Sunday I Spy's voice needed a rest. Instead of singing he sat and watched.

He spied the **ibis ironing** on an **ice-box!**

Can't you see how neatly pressed his feathers are?

ibis

ink

Jj

He spied a **joey jumping** into a pocket.

Check inside your pocket to see if you have any **jumping joeys** inside!

jump

joey

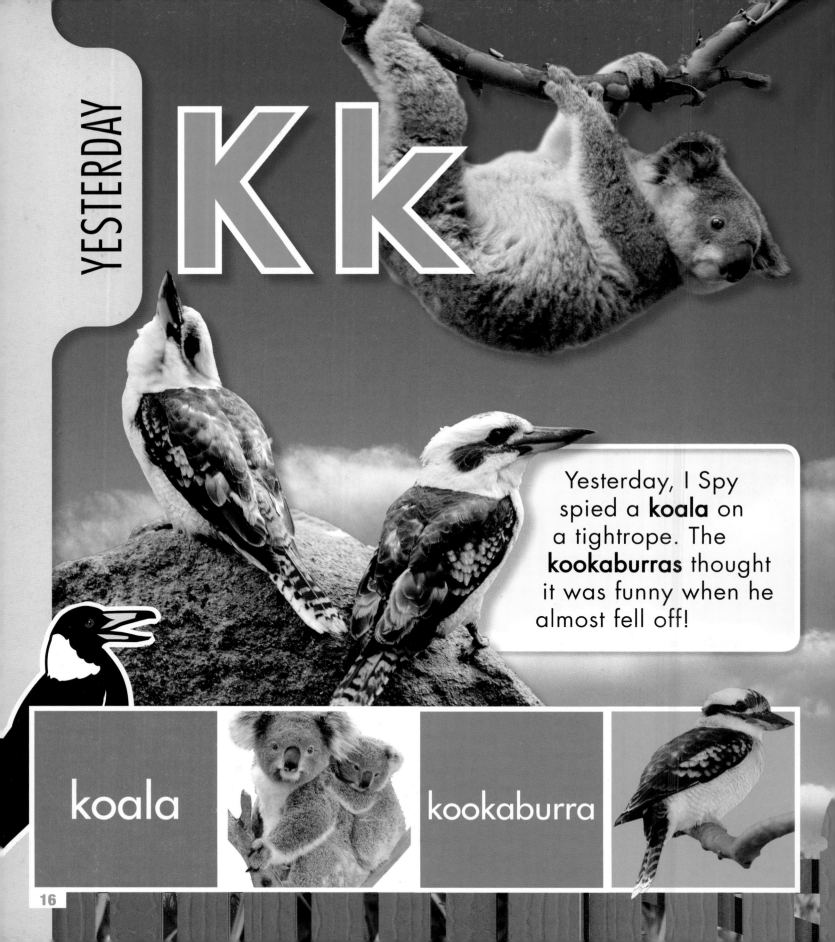

YESTERDAY

Kk

Yesterday, I Spy spied a **koala** on a tightrope. The **kookaburras** thought it was funny when he almost fell off!

koala

kookaburra

Ll

I Spy checked the **letterbox** for **letters** and **listened** to the **lorikeets**.

letter

lorikeet

TODAY

Mm

... what can you see beginning with "M"?

magpie  morning

Nn

Notice his neighbour, Norman, sitting on a "No Standing" sign.

(Norman has the nest next door. Unlike Lori, the neighbour on the other side, Norman never touches the nectar!)

... Now count every "N" (and "n") on this page!

NO STANDING ANY TIME BUSES EXCEPTED

nectar

nest

Tonight while I Spy sleeps, the **owls** are **organising** the **official opening of** the **opera**.

(A gala performance featuring the "hoo's hoo" **of** the **owl** world.)

opera

owl

Pp

I Spy won't see any **possums** tonight!

He won't see any **posts, potatoes, pipes, papers, poultry** or **palm trees**. In fact he won't see anything beginning with "P".

I Spy will be fast asleep!

Can you see anything beginning with "P" when your eyes are closed?

post

palm

Qq

In the morning I Spy got ready for breakfast. He was having cheese and **quackers**, but couldn't find the cheese!

He had plenty of **quackers**.

quack!

quack!

quack!

quack!

quack!

quoll

quail

Rr

Rhyme in the Morning

I Spy woke when **Red Rooster** crowed
and **Ringtail** got **ready** for bed.
Red Rooster recalled how **Ringtail required**
A **rendition** from **rooster** before he **retired**.
Now **repeat** that five times before bed!

rooster

red

NOON

Ss

At noon I Spy **saw** the **sun** high in the **sky**. The **swallows** were **sighing** and the **snails** were **slithering** into the **shadows**.

swallow

snail

Tt

From the **tree-tops** he spied a **tree-frog** praying for rain, a **trespassing toad** and a **tiny turtle taking** a walk.

He invited them in for a cup of "T".

toad

turtle

Uu

In the afternoon, I Spy took a stroll in his **underwear** and put **up** an **umbrella** in case it rained.

Do you like I Spy's **underwear**?

umbrella

underwear

AFTERNOON

Vv

Even though he spent the entire afternoon searching, I Spy couldn't find anything beginning with "V".

Can you see a "V" anywhere?

vine

vase

Ww

One evening I Spy **was walking with Wallaby** and **Wagtail.**

"Why", wondered I Spy, **"would Wagtail wish** to **wander with Wallaby?"**

"Well", whispered Wagtail, "when Wallaby walks, wasps, weevils and **winged** insects take flight and I catch them. **Wallaby** is **wonderful!"**

wheelbarrow

wallaby

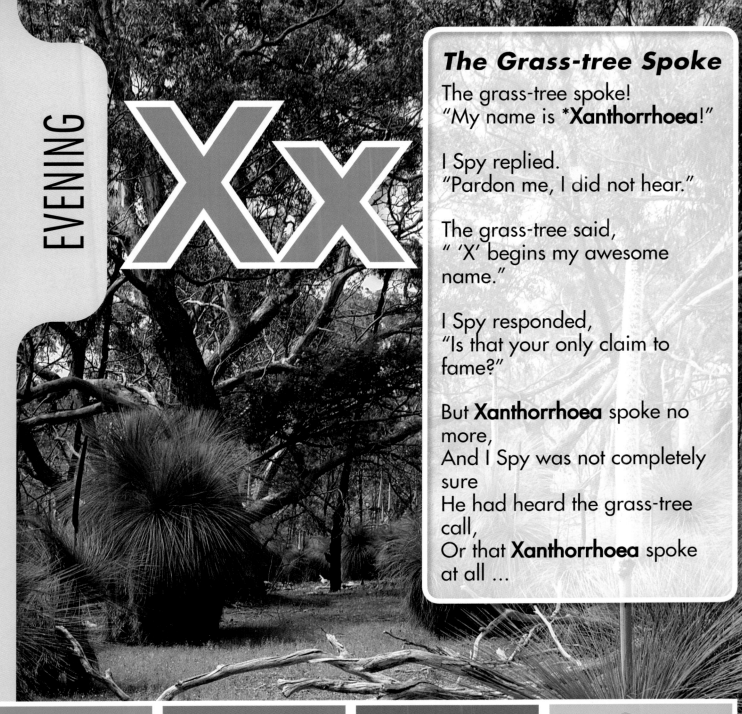

EVENING

Xx

The Grass-tree Spoke

The grass-tree spoke!
"My name is ***Xanthorrhoea**!"

I Spy replied.
"Pardon me, I did not hear."

The grass-tree said,
" 'X' begins my awesome name."

I Spy responded,
"Is that your only claim to fame?"

But **Xanthorrhoea** spoke no more,
And I Spy was not completely sure
He had heard the grass-tree call,
Or that **Xanthorrhoea** spoke at all …

a**x**e

bo**x**

*Pronounced — (zan-thor-rear)

29

Yy

What will I Spy see tomorrow as he sits and peers into my backyard?

He might spy a **yabby** in my **yard**.

He might spy something **yellow** in my **yard**.

He won't see a **yacht** but he might see **you**!

Yawn!

I'm getting tired of thinking about I Spy.

Can you see the letter "Y"?

yellow

yabby

Zz

I think it's time for I Spy and all his friends to go to sleep. Good night!

zebra-crossing

zip

ALL THE TIME IN THE WORLD

I Spy has all the time in the world to learn the alphabet but is he as clever as you are?

Can you say the days of the week?
Do you know the letters of the alphabet?

**Days of
the Week**
Monday, Tuesday,
Wednesday,
Thursday, Friday,
Saturday, Sunday.

**Time of
the Day**
Morning,
Noon, Afternoon,
Evening.

**Past,
Present and
Future**
Yesterday, Today,
Tonight, Tomorrow,
Right Now.

Find Me
There are 45
magpies inside
this book.

Can you find
them all?